Celebrating Tanya Martin Pekel

by Ersula K Odom

Copyright© 2023 Ersula K Odom. All rights reserved. This book may not be reproduced in whole or in part without written permission from the publisher, except by a reviewer who may quote brief passages in a review; nor may any part of this book be reproduced, stored in retrieval system, or transmitted in any form or by any means, electronic, mechanical, photocopying, recording, or other, without written permission from the publisher.

ISBN: 978-1-7365717-9-8
Published 2023
United States

Photographs and documents are courtesy of
Marcia Martin Saunders unless otherwise noted.

Sula Too Publishing
1421 Tampa Park Plaza St
Tampa FL 33605
www.sulatoo.com/publishing

This Commemorative Book
was compiled for a mother with
never ending love and
is Dedicated to:

Marcia Martin Saunders

Montez Martin

Kent Pekel

Lauren Oubre, Adam, & Victoria Pekel

Wendell & Terrie Rayburn

Taylor, Sydney, and Carter Rayburn

Contents

The Beginning	5
Young Tanya	13
Her Break Through Years	23
The Eagle Soars	29
Remembering Tanya	42
Honoring Tanya	60

Tanya Martin-Pekel

The Beginning

When a soft, warm, sweet smelling bundle of joy is placed in a mother's arms for the first time, the impact on the world is like a ripple in an ocean. There is no way to truly measure the distance the ripple will travel and number of lives affected by its waves. On October 3, 1964, Tanya Elayne Martin was put into the arms of her parents, Marcia and Montez Martin creating such an event. We are still experiencing the waves of the incredible impact this child would ultimately have on our society.

1964

Parents

Marcia was from Miami, Florida and Montez was from Columbia, South Carolina. Montez was a Lt. Colonel, Corp of Engineers, stationed in Fort Belvoir, Virginia, where Tanya was born. Marcia and Montez met on Hampton University's campus and were something of a 'star" couple — He was a swimmer and a campus queen. This couple was blessed with two joyful little ones, Tanya and her younger sister Terrie.

Montez and Marcia

Tanya

Terrie

Montez

Parents As Role Models

Montez C. Martin, Jr., Tanya's father's list of accomplishments includes, but not limited to:

President Low Country Housing and Economic Development Foundation, Charleston, South Carolina. He created and operated a 501(C)3 foundation to serve the citizens of the Low Country of South Carolina. He developed performance measures and a Management Team retreat to improve authority operation. Advocates for the Affordable Housing Coalition of South Carolina Mentors youth interns of the Charleston Trident Urban League Member of Charleston Green Committee, which is responsible for developing plans for future land use. He served as a member on the Mayors Council on Homelessness and Affordable Housing. He was a chair of the Board of the Association of Community College Trustees. NAHRO Vice President of Community Revitalization and Development, 2005-2007.

Montez and Tanya

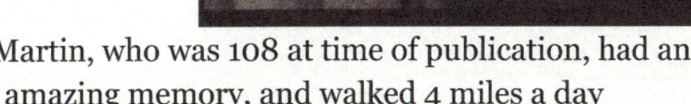

Elise Martin, who was 108 at time of publication, had an amazing memory, and walked 4 miles a day

Tanya's paternal great grandmother, and Elise Martin, her paternal grandmother

Parents As Role Models

Terrie
Marcia & Tanya

During her career, Tanya's mother, Marcia Johnson Martin Saunders, served both as Miami-Dade County's Director of Black Affairs and Miami-Dade County's first Director of the Office of Fair Employment Practices and Diversity Programs reporting directly to esteemed Asst. County Manager Dewey Knight. This office had jurisdiction over resolving discrimination grievances, mediating conflicts and monitoring the County's Affirmative Action Program.

Marcia was member of, or a part of, leadership in countless social and community organizations, among them were:

  Episcopal Church Women
  The Order of the Daughters of the King
  Vestry Board
  All States Tea
  Church Choir
  Dade County Alumnae Chapter
  Delta Sigma Theta Sorority, Inc
  The Links Incorporated of Dade County Chapter
  The United Way
  Urban League of Greater Miami
  International Trade Board
  YWCA
  Family Health Center
  Florida EEO Advisor Committee
  The New Horizons Foundation

Mother's Family

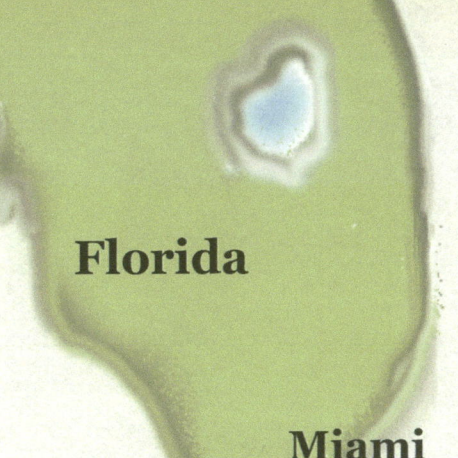

Florida

Miami

Bahama Islands

Tanya's maternal grandmother immigrated from the Bahamas to Florida and worked as a maid in Miami Beach. She wanted her family to have a better life than she did. She wasn't alone. According to Wikipedia, in 1896, foreign-born blacks compromised 40 percent of the black population of Miami, making Miami the largest foreign-born black city in the US aside from New York. Bahamians in Florida created their own institutions, most notably Episcopal churches. During this time in Florida, black Bahamians faced state-enforced racism. Blacks could not vote, were persecuted by epithets in Miami press, and were not allowed to stay in the hotels that employed them. Between 1900 and 1920 between ten and twelve thousand Bahamians moved to Florida, mostly to do agricultural labor, often on a seasonal basis.

Florida farmers convinced the U.S. Congress to exempt Caribbean and Latin American émigrés from the Emergency Quota Act of 1921. In 1921, the Ku Klux Klan staged a large rally attacking these black immigrants in Miami. Starting in 1943, Bahamian workers came to Florida under the British West Indian (BWI) Temporary Labor Program. This program was under the control of private growers from 1947 to 1966. Growers favored Bahamian workers because they "can be forced to work a regular work program or be deported." Racism is a social problem that has plagued the world for centuries. Her grandmother's brush with US Jim Crow laws made their new life in the US "bittersweet" and prompted her parents and generations forward to become involved in the Civil Rights Movement.

1890s-1970s

Northalee Bain Brown & Wardell Brown   Leroy Bain   Young Leroy Bain

Louise Hill Bain

Marcia's mother & father Doris & Donald Johnson

The family story is past on through the ages by family members. Most recently shared by Linda Larry, "Uncle Larry's second daughter FEMA Sheffield" in October 2019. It was told as follows:

William Bain and Louise Hill Bain were married during the late 1890s. Their backgrounds were very different. William was born in the Caribbean island of Nassau, Bahama. Louise was a beautiful, British born, young lady of French descent who spoke French fluently.

William spoke a broken English dialect. He was a tall, dark, and handsome Bohemian man who was also charming, polite, and polished. His behavior was that of a distinguished gentleman. He was a man of a few words, however, when he spoke he had a message and everyone listened. He loved to embrace you with hugs, kisses, and bag of goodies to share. He always had a cheerful smile and was friendly to everyone he met.

William Bain worked on a cruise ship traveling from England to the Bahamas to Florida. Marcia remembers sitting on her great grandfather lap and hearing the elderly Bain shared with her that on one trip there was a horrible hurricane. He made sure that Louise and the person she was traveling with were placed in the safest part of the ship. He brought them food, water and made sure they were ok. By the time they arrived in Dania, he and Louise had bonded. The lady she was traveling with noticed and said she would support his asking her father for her hand in marriage. She did. William then asked for Louise's hand in marriage. She accepted.

Louise's parents lived in England and wanted to meet this young handsome man that their daughter spoke so well of. They were wealthy and could afford to send for him, therefore, they did.

During his visit he was disappointed to learn that his future wife's family did not favor him as their future son-in-law. They told their daughter that they liked him as a person, but his skin color was too black to become a part of their family. Louise's family later disowned her.

William and Louise were married and lived in the United States. During their young married life in America, they experienced racism, segregation, and prejudice. Their lives were bound with fear and worry. Once when William and Louise were out shopping, a white man asked William who was the lady he was with. She had to lie and say that she was a lady he worked for. He never took her out publicly again.

William and Louise began their family. Among their children were Randolph, Charlie, Harold, Herman, Michael, Leroy and Northalee, a daughter. During a fierce storm in 1922, Randolph was swept away in the wind and was never seen again. He was a young teenage boy. Michael was tragically run over by a large truck by a driver who failed to check his surroundings before driving away. Louise also lost other babies through premature birth or miscarriage. She died in childbirth in her mid to early 30s.

William was a hardworking man who tried to keep all of his children together and under one roof, but times were hard, and life became rather overbearing. His burdens became heavy for a young widower and the family separated. The children were split among the extended family who stepped up to give a helping hand. They didn't want the children to go astray nor live from hand to mouth in any way. Harold, as a teenager, became rebellious and William had to assign him to reform school for a short while. Northalee met and married Waddell Brown and they became parents to a daughter, Doris, and a son Howard.

William's siblings were: Abby, a brother; Minerva, a sister; Louise, a sister; Prudence, a sister. There were three sisters and two brothers. Their parents died young in Nassau.

Little information about the people in their line is known. What prevailed was a feeling that family connections were important. It was a celebration of laughter and "catching up on the news" when they came together. They shared whatever they had with each other. They were great cooks and enjoyed the excitement of eating and drinking with each other. It was a party where no one went hungry. You always had to bring something home with you. They were friendly and neighborly and they met no strangers. They cared for the neighborhood children like family. They expressed strong family ties and believed that family is next to God. They were very spiritual, religious, Christian oriented, and God fearing. They were hard workers who were self sufficient and independent. They believed in family unity. They accepted people into their homes and willingly helped them out until they could get out on their own feet. They systematically reared children of alcoholics parents or a father who abandoned their families as well as those who went to prison. They were blessed with many gifts, talents and creativity. The use of their thoughts and talents helped them survive through hard times.

"Jim Crow" laws in the US were a set of state and local laws enacted between 1876 and 1965. These laws had racial segregation as their stated purpose, which was to maintain white supremacy in the southern United States. Rosa Parks is known for her role in ending bus segregation in Montgomery, Alabama. Her actions led to the boycott of Montgomery's city buses by Dr Martin Luther King Jr., who led thousands of African Americans during this period, including students from all-black colleges such as Tuskegee Institute (now University). Rosa Parks' refusal to give up her seat on a city bus sparked an entire movement that changed history forever...the Civil Rights Movement! The Movement benefited Tanya personally because she was afforded the opportunity to attend "sparsely integrated schools." Tanya was also exposed to a world view given that during her childhood Tanya and her younger sister Terrie spent summers in the Bahamas.

Tanya and Terrie

When Tanya was six, her mother relocated Tanya and her sister to Miami and reared them as a single mother. She enrolled them in the Miami Dade County Public Schools. Ultimately, she attended Morningside Elementary School, Miami Shores Elementary School, Horace Mann Junior High School, North Miami Middle School and North Miami Sr. High School.

Tanya and Terrie were imbued with the immigrant penchant for hard work and an appreciation for education.
When enrolling Tanya in Phyllis Wheatley Public School, the school secretary stated she would be in first grade. Her mother repeatedly stated that Tanya could read. Overhearing the issue Mrs Albert, the principal retrieved several books from nearby shelves and instructed Tanya to read whichever book she desired. Upon hearing Tanya read, the principal placed her in second grade.

The photo on the right was taken after Terrie and Tanya were confirmed at the Episcopal Church of the Incarnation. The church played a major role in both of the girl's development.

Terrie and Tanya

Young Tanya

Young Tanya

Personal

Name: Tanya Elayne Martin
Address: 8915 NW 10th ave
Phone: 696-2087
Age: seventeen
Height: five feet four 5'4"
Weight:

Favorite:
Hobbies: Piano, flute, reading, writing, music
Songs: Teach Me, Rosanna, If You Could Read My Mind, Endless Love, Love Song, Wherever She Is, Closer to Your Love, Blue
Colors: lavender, blue
Other: favorites: musicals, poetry, reggae, pop, jazz

EVALUATION
PROGRESS SHEET

KINDERGARTEN

Columbia College
Columbia, South Carolina 29203

Child's name: TANYA MARTIN
Date: MAY 27, 1970
Days present: 165
Days absent: 13

Metropolitan Readiness Test: SUPERIOR

Physical Development:

Tanya enjoys good health and has a good body build. Is left-handed. Has excellent coordination and manual dexterity. She is very active always — indoors and outdoors.

Social Development:

Tanya knows exactly what, when, and where things should be done. Routine and rules are fixed in her mind, and she tends to become impatient with those who do not do as they should. She takes her responsibilities seriously. One can depend on her always. She tends to be a perfectionist and that keeps her from having a peaceful relationship with others at all times. Loves and respects her teachers, who love her, also.

Emotional Development:

Tanya has progressed a great deal in the control of her emotions. She is a happy child and has consideration for herself and others, even though at times she has conflicts with others. Most of the time she is right in the conflicts, and defends her rights to the end. She just needs to calm down to be able to get her point accross. She also becomes very excited over something she likes, and almost loses control. We have to be careful not to over-stimulate her.

Intellectual Development:

Tanya has a keen mind. Her English is excellent, and she is often correcting others: " You don't say 'ain't it'; you say 'isn't it'". Also, " There is no such word as 'you all'; it's just ' you ' ". She is certainly interested in all language skills — stories, books, writing, copying, counting, telling stories

Tanya's Kindergarten assessment

Young Tanya

Tanya's schedule showed she was a voracious reader and a regular at her local library. Her mom said she read the Miami Herald every morning.

Tanya and two other North Miami students competed for 5,000 National Merit Scholarships offered in 1982 to those semifinalists who became finalists. These semifinalists represented the top one-half percent of the state's high school senior class.

During her middle and high school years, Tanya was involved in a plethora of community organizations including Girl Scouts & Band; penned a weekly Teen Talk article for the Miami Times; volunteer with the American Cancer Society; dance student with the Florine Nichols Dance Studio; active in the youth ministry at the Episcopal Church of the Incarnation; played flute in the North Miami Senior High School marching band; participated in the Fine Arts Club; National Honor Society, and was one of 3 merit scholars from Dade County. Another reference said she was one of 3 National Merit semi-finalists. Tanya graduated with honors in 1982. Her list of Senior Activities was impressive:

- Sophomore Class Treasurer
- Honor Guard
- Preps
- Prom Page
- Junior and Senior Advisory Boards
- Concert Band
- Science Honor Society
- Paramed Secretary
- 1981 Prom Chairman
- Fine Arts Secretary
  Pioneer Regiment Guard Flag Lieutenant
- Spanish National Honor Society

- ICC
- Beta National Honor Society
- SHCOG Secretary,
- State Band
- SG Delegate
- Fine Arts President
- National Honor Society - Vice President
- National Achievement Semi Finalist
- Super Senior
- Miss Conestoga nominee
- National Merit Semi Finalist

1974-1982

NORTH MIAMI DADE

Baby Pioneers hurry to elect officers

Baby Pioneers got off to a quick start this year when they elected officers to serve them. Led by new sponsor, Mrs. Laurie Foreman, this group of special students helped the Sophomore Class to have its most successful year in a long time.

Baby Pioneer officers who worked with Mrs. Foreman were Jeff Zucker, president; Janice Raiford, vice-president; Lisa Pare, corresponding secretary; Robin Krinsky, recording secretary, and Tanya Martin, treasurer.

All of the tenth grade candidates seeking office were highly qualified. Each candidate had to have good grades and teacher recommendations. Those students who ran but were not elected were Howard Stolar, Linda Sils, Michele Goldin, Michelle Camp, Lisa Specter, and Carol Neu.

Treasurer elect Tanya Martin awaits her turn to speak.

Teen Talk
By Tanya Martin

Most of Dade Schools are celebrating Black History month this week.

Here is a history quiz, see how well you do. Answers at end of article.

1. What is the name of the ... and a founder of Kwanza, 7. Jesse Jackson, 8. Barbara Jordan, 9. Ambassador to the U.N., 10. Edward Brookes, 11. John H. Johnson, 12. North Carolina Mutual, 13. Motown Records, 14. Hank Aaron, 15.

Tanya penned a weekly Teen Talk article for the Miami Times

PIONEER REGIMENT: (front) Tanya Martin, Flag Lieutenant; Irene Trousbridge, Guard Captain; (back) Lisa Ventervogel, Cindy Binder, Wendy Specter, Marian Klement, Cecily Robinson, Ann Moore, Kara MacCullough, Caryn Shirley, and Tina DiPrima.

Tanya & Congressman William Lehman

Florida Legislative Pages

Shortly after a 1980 visit to the Florida Capitol with North Miami High School tenth grade class, Tanya met Congressman William Lehman. He spoke at the Miami Dade Commission. At the end of the meeting, the fires were burning from the McDuffie Riots. Congressman Lehman's staff person was unsure of the best way to get to Miami Beach without crossing Biscayne Bay from down town.

Marcia suggested that he cross over at 125st. He seemed confused, so Marcia suggested he follow her and she would direct him further. When they safely passed the fire area, she pulled over and showed them the short distance they would have to travel. Congressman Lehman said, "No, we will see that you get home safely first."

When she pulled into her driveway, her daughters, Tanya and Terrie, came out to greet them. When Marcia introduced them to Congressman Lehman, Tanya expressed how excited she and her classmates' visit to the State Capitol. She shared how honored she was to meet him. They talked briefly and he suggested if she was interested to apply for a White House Page, which she did and was appointed. Tanya served as a page for U.S. Representative William Lehman.

1974-1982

Published in the Prometheus Black - a publication of the Black Student Alliance of Duke University, Durham, N.C.

COLOURS

She said, look you ole colored girl
and I took offense, only at the word "girl,"
for I am a woman,
and I said,
Colour me
and my people everywhere.
Colour me blue,
like the tears that were shed
as we crossed the oceans, in changes
Colour me red,
the shade of my blood
that has been spilled in search of freedom.
Colour me yellow,
brighter than any sun
or the gold, to which I am the rightful owner.
Colour me brown,
a deep, rich, tint
like that of the life nourishing soil.
Colour me purple,
royal, that is,
as our souls know we were meant to be; indeed
colour me all these colors;
mix them together;
and you color me black
no create heritage does exist!
Yes, I am colored.
What color are you?   Tanya Elayne Martin

In Her Own Words

Duke Teaches More Than Class Facts
By Tanya Martin

We come to you tonight through a scorching fire
A fire that continually threatens our unique art

Yet, flames cannot burn creativity
Nor can they smite dedication or destroy beauty

Our history shows that
We will overcome any obstacle
Any fire

I wrote this poem for the "Dance Black" recital "Through the Fire," but it reminds me of being here at Duke - in particular, being a black student at Duke. We are often engaged in a struggle to keep our cultural background and identity alive at Duke. It is difficult, and perhaps rewarding, to maintain groups such as Karamu when Duke's black population is so very minute.

There exist at Duke a misconception that the black students are a monolithic, separatist group. It simply is not true. The only thing that we have in common is that blacks are often the victims of prejudice, injustice, and isolation, all on the basis of skin color. Not always recognized is that black Americans share a unique culture one that is often overlooked. I was asked to write comments that were inclusive of the experience of black students at Duke. While many of my racial peers will see parts of their Duke story in mine, I can only speak to one black experience, my own.

First printed in 1986 Duke yearbook.

1982 -1986

Tanya wrote:

I recently completed my term as president of the Black Student Alliance, a group sometimes criticized for promoting segregation in the Duke community. But to those who suggest that the BSA promotes a cultural separation, I reply that the BSA is not the cause of black culture, instead it is the manifestation of black culture at Duke. I think that it is a great thing for us to have on campus the mechanisms to learn about people different from ourselves. This is something I have tried to take advantage of these last four years, and some of the most meaningful things I have learned have been in the living classroom of Duke community. And sometimes it is difficult not to feel like a living curiosity exhibit when people have asked sensitive questions. However, the alternative of allowing ignorance to continue to flourish is much worse.

I have tried to learn not only about my fellow classmates but my fellow Durham residents. I feel that I have a responsibility to the community I live in, and that includes Durham as well as Duke. I have never lived off campus, but neither have I hid for four years behind our infamous gothic walls.

Reaching out to help others is the fundamental part of the black Greek tradition, therefore, in my sophomore year I pledged Delta Sigma Theta Sorority. Many of my friends did not understand the concept of "on line." Pledging is a process of learning how to function in a group to reach a common goal, and building a bond of sisterhood and love that is in eternal. Our commitment to service extends past our Duke lives. My sorority, as with other black Greek organizations, has active graduate chapters and that will give me the opportunity to always give to those who have not been as fortunate as I am.

Like every other senior, I do not know what I will be doing when I see this issue of the Chanticleer. However, I am sure that I will appreciate even more the experience I have had and the friends that I have made while I was here. I do not expect to remember all of the classroom facts, but I have learned how to think and to question and form my own beliefs. There is not any greater lesson to be learned. Most of all, I am glad I have had the chance to be and deal with Dukies. I think we are a unique student body, and I am proud to be a "Cameron sixth man." It is, it has been fun, and I'll take with me all the things it meant to be a Blue Devil; the kinds of people we all were, and how we expressed ourselves. It will always be a part of me. Yes, things could have been better, but things weren't so bad at all.

Tonya Martin held the position of BSA president in 1985.

1982 -1986

Her Break Through Years

Her Break Through Years

Duke University 1982-1986 AB Economics; Recruited by Duke as a high school senior. While at Duke: made the dean's list; performed with Dance Black; sang with Modern Black Mass Choir; published her poems in Prometheus Black (journal published by black students at Duke); pledged Delta Sigma Theta and her Lambda Omega Chapter served the wider Durham community; was president of the Black Student Alliance and served on the President's Honor Council; member of Duke University Black Alumni Connection; 1986 class representative; Reunion Coordinator; chaired a recruitment committee for the admissions office; danced with a modern/jazz group; worked in the Durham community via campus outreach organizations to mentor young Durham students.

After graduation, she spent a summer teaching at the University of Miami's Upward Bound program. As an Economic Opportunity Act of 1964 Federal program founded August 26, 1965, Upward Bound provides fundamental support to participants in their preparation for college entrance. The program provides opportunities for participants to succeed in their precollege performance and ultimately in their higher education pursuits. Upward Bound serves: high school students from low-income families; and high school students from families in which neither parent holds a bachelor's degree. The goal of Upward Bound is to increase the rate at which participants complete secondary education and enroll in and graduate from institutions of postsecondary education.

Duke University School of Law. 1986-1989 (JD). Was the recipient of a tuition scholarship and directed the Volunteer Income Tax Assistance program. Was secretary of the Duke Bar and coordinator of the minority recruitment weekend.

1982 -1986

Duke University

The Faculty and Trustees in recognition of the successful completion of the course of study required by the

Trinity College of Arts and Sciences

have conferred on

Tanya Elayne Martin

the degree of

Bachelor of Arts

Given at Durham in the State of North Carolina this fourth day of May, one thousand nine hundred and eighty-six.

Chairman of Board of Trustees

President of the University

R. A. White
Dean

Roger L. Marshall
Secretary of the University

Career Begins

Tanya's professional career began as a corporate attorney at Simpson, Thatcher & Bartlett on Wall Street 1989. While there she provided pro-bono services to the Friends of the Dance Theater of Harlem and the Volunteer Lawyers for the Arts. Simpson Thatcher was founded in 1884. The company built a worldwide presence with ten offices and more than 1,000 lawyers.

Tanya moved to Los Angeles and worked for Southern California Edison as an attorney specializing in nuclear licensing and waste disposal matters. She won the company's "Corporate Award for Superior Performance" three years in a row. At that time, Southern California Edison was the largest subsidiary of Edison International and the primary electricity supply company for much of Southern California. It provided 14 million people with electricity across a service territory of approximately 50,000 square miles.

She also volunteered with an inner city LA children's ministry teaching Sunday school, SAT classes, and modern dance. She was involved in local bar associations and the Junior League.

1989

Family Life

Marriage & Motherhood

Tanya married Derek Oubre in 1990. They had one daughter, Lauren.

She found her "soulmate" in her second husband, Kent Pekel. Both were described as "insular" but they were able to open up to each other. He was from Bloomington, Minnesota, a social studies teacher at a local high school who also coordinated a summer teaching program in Shanghai, China. He was in her class of White House Fellows and they married in 1999. They had a son, Adam and a daughter, Victoria.

Tanya was described as a "practical" parent, focussed on the things that mattered and didn't sweat the small stuff. Reading to her children was important. A home cooked meal not so much. She was not averse to ordering out.

At publication, there were videos on YouTube: one of their daughter singing—Victoria Pekel— and one Kent made on the 10th anniversary of Tanya's death—(Glimpses of Tanya Pekel).

1990-1999

*"Granny,
Here's your first picture"*

The Waves

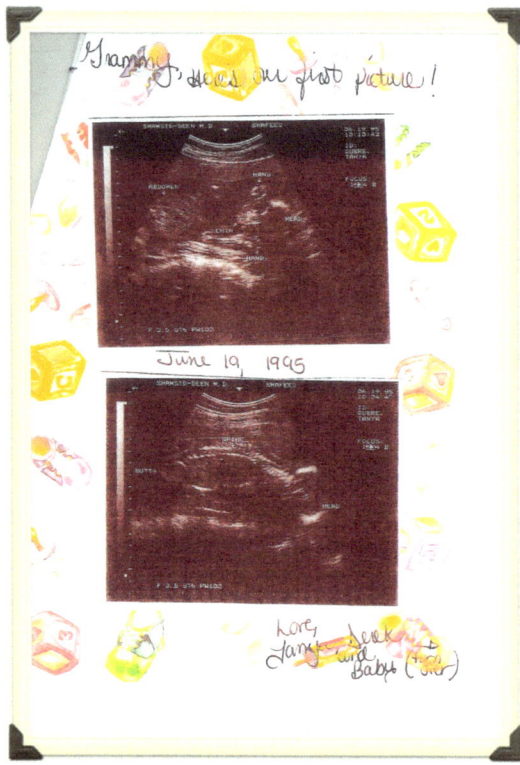

HER DAUGHTER: https://www.youtube.com/watch?v=MEpu_VNpf7I

HER FAMILY: https://www.youtube.com/watch?v=kSDBOWeVhJc&t=252s
"This video shows her at home with her children Lauren, Adam, and Victoria, and ends with a segment of the speech she gave at her sister Emily's high school graduation. Just a few glimpses of the amazing woman she was." -- Kent

Lauren, Kent, Tanya, Adam, Victoria

1995

The Eagle Soars

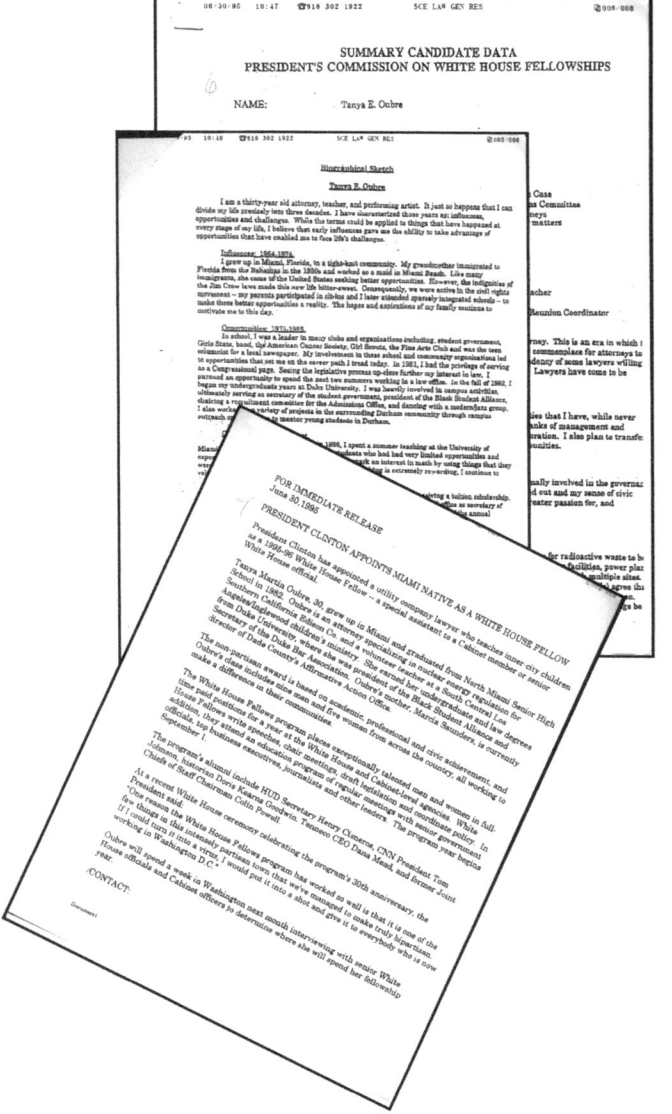

FOR IMMEDIATE RELEASE
June 30, 1995
PRESIDENT CLINTON APPOINTS MIAMI NATIVE AS A WHITE HOUSE FELLOW

President Clinton has appointed a utility company lawyer who teaches inner-city children as a 1995-96 White House Fellow -- a special assistant to a Cabinet member or senior White House official.

Tanya Martin Oubre, 30, grew up in Miami and graduated from North Miami Senior High School in 1982. Oubre is an attorney specializing in nuclear energy regulation for Southern California Edison Co. and a volunteer teacher at a South Central Los Angeles/Inglewood children's ministry. She earned her undergraduate and law degrees from Duke University, where she was president of the Black Student Alliance and Secretary of the Duke Bar Association. Oubre's mother, Marcia Saunders, is currently director of Dade County's Affirmative Action Office.

The non-partisan award is based on academic, professional and civic achievement, and Oubre's class includes nine men and five women from across the country, all working to make a difference in their communities.

The White House Fellows program places exceptionally talented men and women in full time paid positions for a year at the White House and Cabinet-level agencies. White House Fellows write speeches, chair meetings, draft legislation and coordinate policy. In addition, they attend an education program of regular meetings with senior government officials, top business executives, journalists and other leaders. The program year begins September 1.

The program's alumni include HUD Secretary Henry Cisneros, CNN President Tom Johnson, historian Doris Kearns Goodwin, Tenneco CEO Dana Mead, and former Joint Chiefs of Staff Chairman Colin Powell.

1995

At a White House ceremony celebrating the program's 30th anniversary, the President said:

"One reason the White House Fellows program has worked so well is that it is one of the few things in this intensely partisan town that we've managed to make truly bipartisan. If I could turn it into a virus, I would put it in a shop and give it to everyone who is now working in Washington, D.C."

"Oubre will spend a week in Washington next month interviewing with senior White House officials and Cabinet office to determine where she will spend her fellowship year."

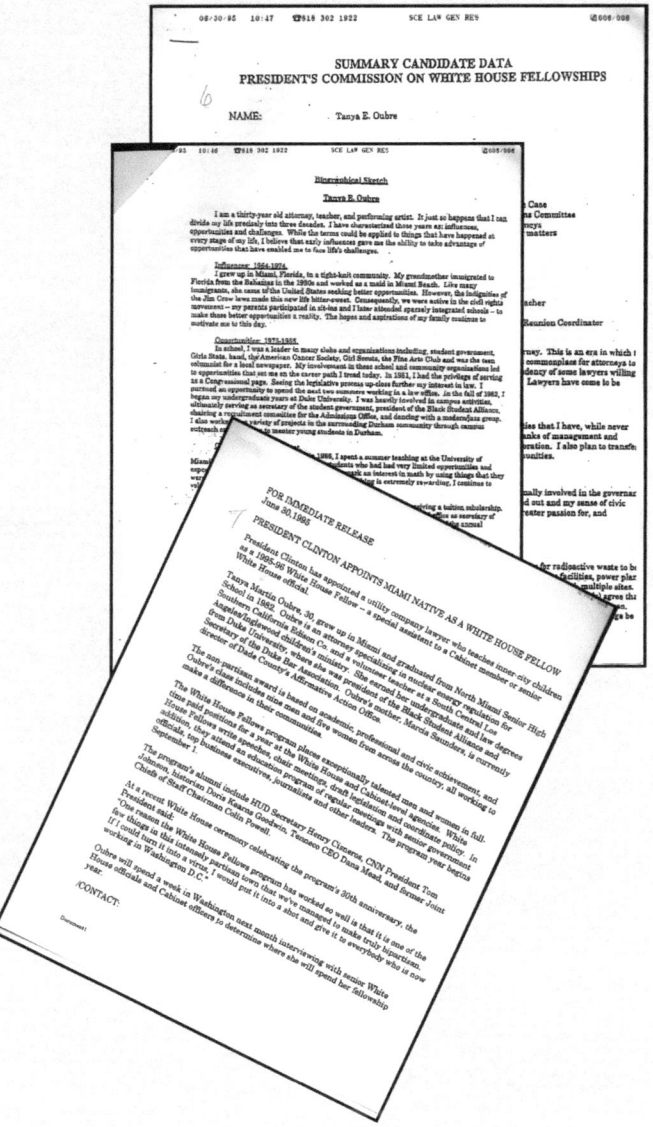

1995

*To Tanya Martin Oubre
With Appreciation,*

President William Jefferson Clinton & Tanya

Tanya E. Martin
Associate Director for Education and Policy Planning
Domestic Policy Council

The White House

(202) 456-5228
Fax: (202) 456-5581

White House Fellows Class of 1995 - 1996

David E. Jones, 33 Sacramento, California; attorney withLegal Services on Northern California, Inc. and board member of the Sacramento Mutual Housing Association.

Teresa Leggier de Fernandez, 35, Sante Fe, New Mexico; attorney with the firm of Nordhaus, Haltom, Taylor & Frye, specializing in the representation of Native America tribes.

Robert W. Leland, 32, Albuquerque, New Mexico; senior staff member at Sandia National Laboratories and volunteer math and science public school teacher.

Peter Lawrence Levin, 33, Worcester, Massachusetts; associate professor of electrical and computer engineering at Worcester Polytechnic Institute and founder of a community recycling program.

Cynthia McCaffrey, 29, Austin, Texas; graduate student at the LBJ School of Public Affairs and founder of school in Malawi for vulnerable children.

Tanya E. Oubre, 30, Los Angeles, California; attorney with Southern California Edison Company and children's dance teacher.

Kent Pekel, 27, Bloomington, Minnesota; social studies teacher at Thomas Jefferson High School and coordinates a summer teaching program in Shanghai, China.

Anthony D. So, 34, Philadelphia, Pennsylvania; medical research associate, American College of Physicians and principal organizer of Asian American Health Care Network.

Julia C. Vindasius, 33, Pine Bluff, Arkansas; executive director of the Good Faith Fund and board member of Pine Bluff Downtown Development organization.

King Zalesne, 29, Philadelphia, Pennsylvania; assistant district attorney and cantor of the Society Hill Synagogue.

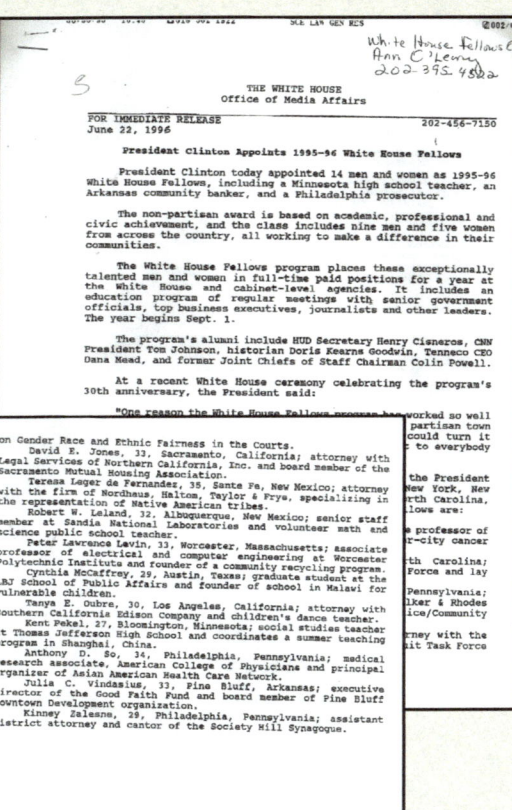

1995 - 1996

From Florida, to California, Washington DC, and Minnesota

In 1999, following her appointment as a White House Fellow, Tanya moved to Minneapolis and became Chief Of Staff (COS) for the St. Paul Schools Superintendent, Patricia Harvey. St. Paul's schools serviced over 44,000 students. As COS, Tanya "shaped and steered an improvement agenda that became a national model for urban education reform. She was particularly central to reforms in the district's organizational structure. She conceived and led St. Paul Public Schools' nationally recognized effort to decentralize resources and decision-making authority to the school level, with a district-wide system of support and accountability for results. The results: According to the DC-based Council of the Great City Schools, during Tanya's tenure the St. Paul Public Schools made more progress in closing the achievement gap between white and students whose first language is not English than any other large district in the country. During her tenure, 3rd graders in St. Paul made 11 times more progress than the average of other large US school districts and 5th graders made more than 20 times more progress than the average of other large districts. Overall during Tanya's tenure, the 1% of elementary school students in St. Paul who scored proficient in reading and math doubled —from approximately 1/3 to 23. High School graduation rates increased by 6%. She shaped and led dramatic changes."

1999

White House Fellows Class: Nomination of Tanya Martin Pekel, 1995-1996 for the John W. Gardner of Leadership Award

Navigating by Mountains

(June 30 2006)

Introduction

"Tanya Martin Pekel accomplished more in her 42 years than most people do who get 80."

A corporate attorney, a domestic policy expert, an urban-school innovator, a loving mother of three, and the glue of every community she joined - Tanya Pekel was the model of what John Gardner envisioned for the White House Fellows. Her death following a two-and-a-half-year battle with cancer, triggered one of our community's great losses.

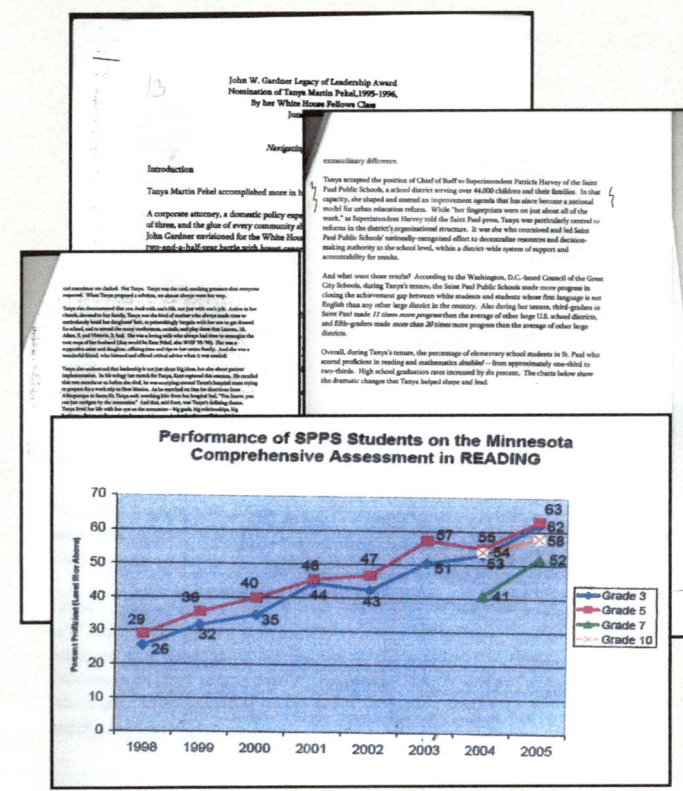

White House Fellows Class 2006

Professional Achievement

After graduating from Duke Law School in 1989, Tanya joined the leading law firm of Simpson. Thatcher and Bartlett in New York. She later moved to the Counsel's Office of the Southern California Edison Company, where she specialized in the highly charged field of nuclear licensing and waste disposal matters, and won the company's "Corporate Award for Superior Performance three years in a row. Tanya's skill at managing and navigating complex. high-stakes issues could have propelled her to the top of the corporate bar. But Tanya's heart was in education. Having been raised by a single mother who insisted she never sell herself short Tanya was determined that every child have the chance to be his or her best.

As a White House Fellow in 1995-1996. Tanya had the chance to follow this passion. Tanya worked for Secretary Dick Riley at the Department of Education where she quickly proved her ability to identify challenges and brainstorm solutions. Combining her well-honed analytical talent with her new understanding of federal education policy, Tanya rapidly became a dignified and effective advocate for children in every corner of the country.

The White House noticed. When her Fellowship ended, the head of President Clinton's Domestic Policy Council ask Tanya to serve as the President's Associate Director for Education Policy and Planning. In that role, she helped shape the key education initiatives of the turn of the century -- *class* size reduction. volunteer service, school construction, bilingual education, and charter school development.

In 1999, Tanya left the White House on exactly the trajectory John Gardner envisioned: to take the. lessons of federal service back to the community level, where she could make an extraordinary difference.

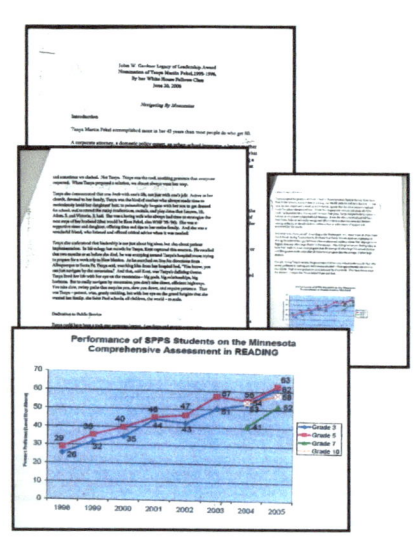

White House Fellows Class

2006

Tanya accepted the position of chief of staff to Superintendent Patricia Harvey of the Saint Paul public schools, a school district serving over 44,000 children and their families. In that capacity, she shaped and steered and improvement agenda that has since become a national model for urban education reform. While "her fingerprints were on just about all of the work," as Superintendent Harvey told the Saint Paul press, Tanya was particularly central to reforms in a district's organizational structure. It was she who conceived and led Saint Paul Public Schools nationally recognized effort to decentralized resources and decision making authority to the school level within a district wide system of support and accountability for results.

And what were the results? According to the Washington DC-based Council of the Great City Schools during Tanya's tenure, the Saint Paul public schools made more progress in closing the gap between white students and students whose first language is not English than any of the large district in the country. Also during Tanya's tenure, third graders in Saint Paul made 11 times more progress than the average of other large US school districts and fifth graders made more than 20 times more progress than the average of other large districts overall.

Overall, during Tanya's tenure, the percentage of elementary school students in Saint Paul who scored proficient in reading and mathematics doubled — from approximately one-third to two-thirds. High school graduation rates increase by six percent. The chart below shows the dramatic changes that Tanya helped shape and lead.

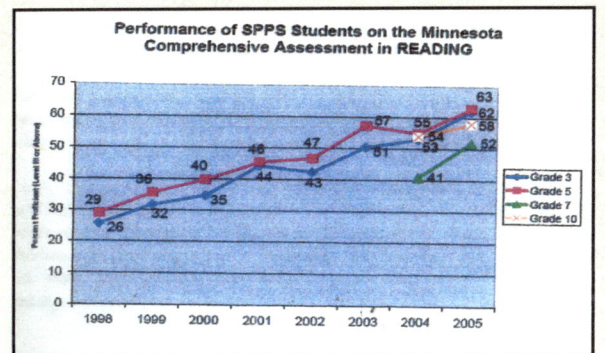

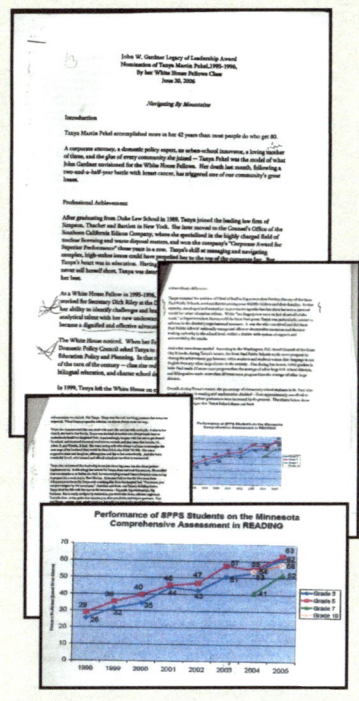

White House Fellows Class

2006

These and other educational improvements made under Tanya's leadership in Saint Paul are particularly striking because during her tenure, the percentage of students who faced significant educational challenges (including living in poverty, having a first language other than English or being disabled) went dramatically up. in addition, during this period, the district was forced by state funding shortfalls and declining enrollment to reduce its budget by over $80 million. With patience wisdom and great creativity Tanya guided the district through those challenges an accomplished the remarkable improvements named above.

Those statistics are remarkable. Even better, behind every one of them is a child, an American, a future adult who will now be able to contribute to the safety, prosperity, and integrity of our nation.

Her chosen community took notice. In 2000, Tanya was named one of Minneapolis St. Paul's "100 People to Watch." In 2003, she was featured in Saint Paul's Pioneer Press special section on "A few of Tomorrow's Leaders Today."

Said Harvey at Tanya's funeral, "Tanya was a source of peace. She could and did do everything. She never wanted the spotlight. She'd have liked to be invisible. But giants are not invisible.

Leadership

Tanya's professional success flowed directly from her natural leadership abilities. It is said that the hallmark of a great leader is unwavering respect for the people she leads. Tanya had a deep wellspring of respect for everyone she encountered. Maybe it was from having such diverse personal ties --- from her mother's Bahamas to her father's South Carolina, from her childhood Florida to her professional New York and California,

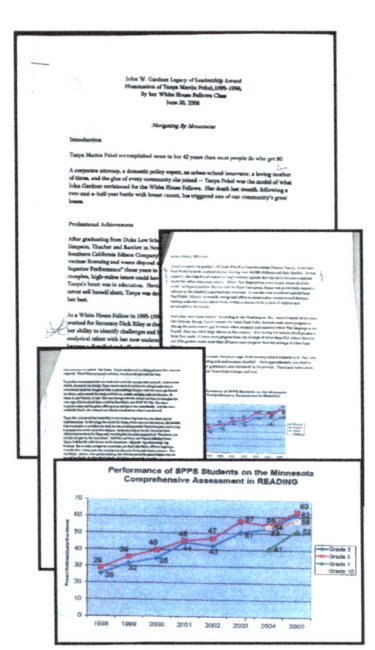

White House Fellows Class

2006

from her fellowship in Washington, DC, to her husband's hometown Saint Paul -- Tanya was a little bit of all of America. That she "represented" America was taken to its height during the Fellow's trip to Vietnam. As she walked through Hanoi, two Vietnamese boys saw Tanya and yelled out, "Janet Jackson! Janet Jackson!" A devoted pop culture fan, Tanya was perhaps never so happy.

Maybe her leadership ability came from an ability to connect to people on such a low-key, personal level. Mary Cathryn Ricker, president of the Saint Paul Federation of Teachers, recalled that when she first met Tanya, Tanya put her right at ease by talking about their shared experience as working mothers. Despite Tanya's impressive title and credentials, Richter said, "She was the least pretentious person I think I have ever met."

One of Tanya's unique and quite incredible qualities was her gentle, persuasive ability to lead discussions exactly where they needed to go. Our fellows class had lots of hot personalities, and sometimes we clashed, not Tonya. Tonya was the cool soothing presence that everyone respected. When Tonia proposed a solution we almost always win her way.

Tanya also demonstrated that one leads with one's life not just with one's job. She was active in her church and devoted to her family. She was confirmed as a child and very active math the Episcopal Church. Tanya was the kind of mother who always made time to meticulously braid her daughter's hair, to bargain with her son to get dressed for school, and to attend the mini conferences, recitals, and play dates that Lauren, Tim, Adam, and Victoria. She was a loving wife who always had time to strategize the next steps of her husband (that would be Kent Pekel), also WHF 9596. She was a supportive sister and daughter, offering time and tips to her entire family, and as she was a wonderful friend who listened and offered advice when it was needed.

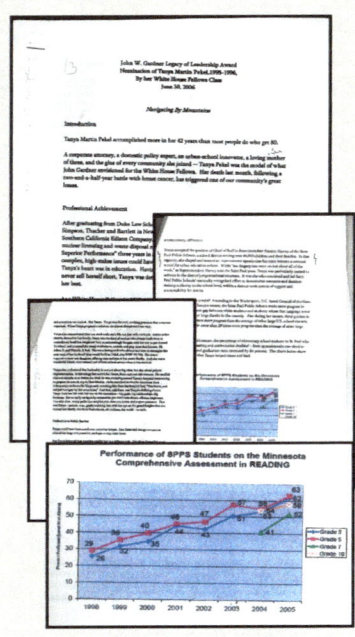

White House Fellows Class

2006

Tanya also understood that leadership is not just about big ideas, but also about patient implementation. In his eulogy for Tanya, Kent captured this essence. He recalled that two months or so before she died, he was scurrying around Tanya's hospital bed room trying to prepare for a work trip to New Mexico. As he searched online for directions from Albuquerque to Santa Fe Tanya said, watching him from her hospital bed, "You know you can just navigate by the mountains." And that, said Kent, was Tanya's defining theme. Tanya lived her life with her eyes on the mountains - big goals big relationships big horizons. But to really navigate by mountains, you don't take the direct, efficient highways. You take slow, twisty paths that surprise you, slowdown you down, and require patience. That was Tanya - patient, wises, gently trekking, but with her eyes on the grand heights that she wanted her family, the Saint Paul schools, all children, the world – to scale.

Dedication to public service

Tanya could have been a rockstar corporate lawyer. Law firms and energy companies offered her large compensation packages to stay with them.

What time you believe that American needed her in a different room. She chose instead to go to St. Paul, to manage the daily, unglamorous, but critical functions of a middle America school system. And she did it with a success that you and Ervin * school. Tanya's commitment to public service was from a young age venturing from Miami to Washington DC to serve as a congressional page in high school public service. Throughout her life she taught music, drama, and dance to children inner city ministry in addition she volunteered as a tutor and mentor at four at risk youth. These activities are typical of Tanya, she was always a doer. She led by quiet and dignified example.

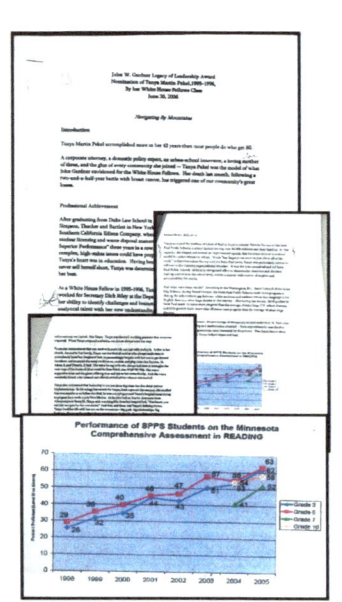

White House Fellows Class

2006

Support to the White House Fellows Community

As a White House Fellow, Tanya was the nurturing presence that brought our desperate group together. She was the "source of peace" for us too when we needed it most. And for the 10 years since our Fellowship ended, Tanya was always Tonya and has always been the one to keep us in touch. Somehow among the demands of a full time, high-profile job; birthing an raising three children; and being married to a frenetically brilliant man (Kent, as we mentioned), Tanya still managed to send out regular newsletters on our classmates whereabouts, and to diligently keep us all connected. She is the one who organized our video yearbook and updated it last October - in between chemo treatments - for our 10-year anniversary. Tanya was perhaps the person with the least amount of extra time in a day, but she did it because it was truly important to her.

Post-Fellowship, Tanya has been a steady resource for Entering Fellows on how to balance the great opportunities of the program with the real demands of the rest of life. Probably the first in the history of the Fellowship to give birth while a Fellow – Tanya became a tried-and-true expert on how to balance everything. A full decade of Fellows classes have now turned to Tanya for warm candid incredibly helpful advice on integrating the Fellowship into the rest of life.

Conclusion

Our only regret in submitting this letter is that we are not able to do it decades from now, when Tanya's personal and professional leadership would have taken even greater hold.

We imagine that when John Gardner envisioned the model White House Fellow, he imagined a person of humble roots and great accomplishment, devoted to family and doing the unglamorous, but vital work of helping America fulfill his great potential. Tanya Martin Pekel was that Fellow. We are honored to submit this letter, and grateful for having been her friends.

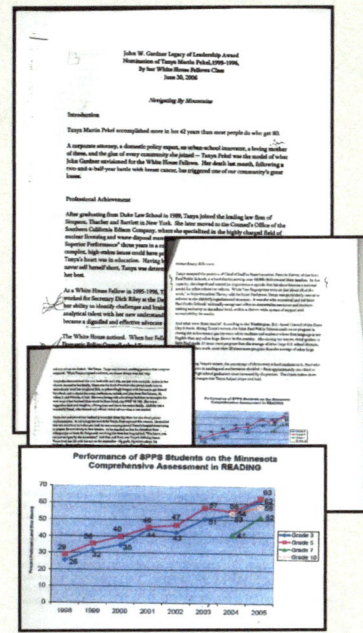

White House Fellows Class

2006

Remembering Tanya

Her Personality

Remembering Tanya

Tanya's personality becomes clear as we read the words of her family, friends and co-workers. These are the words that linger:

- Tanya was described by a friend as a woman who had achieved "balance", a woman of many gifts who did not let anyone dominate her.

- She was understated; didn't draw attention to herself; her knowledge base from reading and from her teachers was broad; she had an analytical mind.

- Didn't particularly care about outward appearances, though she was neat, or cared about fashion. Her beauty was within. She was a good friend. Available when you needed her.

- She was her "own person...direct..forthright and without any show of pomposity.

- "She was headstrong and no-nonsense."

- "She led by quiet and dignified example. She demonstrated that one leads with one's life, not just one's job.

- Even while juggling her chemotherapy treatments, doctor's appointments, work and caring for her family....she never complained.

- Sent her mom a copy of her ultra sound of her baby with a note: "The first installment of your brag book... the baby is fine but moves a lot—so we couldn't get a real good 'face' shot." Photo of ultra sound

- "Tanya was a little bit of all of America."

- Many of the documents these excerpts were taken from are contained on the upcoming pages. You may find it interesting to discover them within the context they were shared. asked what her significant contribution to her professional field on the Summary Candidate Data President's Commission on White House Fellows form she said: " My most significant contribution to my field is being a competent and ethnical attorney...Today, it is commonplace for attorneys to be fodder in a stand up comic's or even an office comic's routine...the tendency of some lawyers willing to argue any point, no matter how ludicrous, seemingly justifies the harsh criticism. Lawyers have come to be viewed as cynical hired guns who will support anything for the right price."

- Tanya also stated: "Professionally, my goal is to climb the ranks of management and ultimately become the general counsel or a senior executive officer of a major corporation......I also plan to transfer (my) business skills and expertise to support economic ventures in disadvantaged communities."

Remembering Tanya

Dr. Patricia Harvey, Rosemary Enslin, Tanya

"Every time a child in the city of Saint Paul picked up a book, Tanya Martin Pekel's fingerprints were somewhere on that book too." Dr. Patricia Harvey

For many of us, the passing of Dr. Patricia Harvey marks a transition that is both personal and professional. This picture shows Pat and my wife Tanya, who was her Chief-of-Staff in the school district, with Rosemary Enslin, who was an amazing executive assistant for both of them. When this picture was taken, Tanya was in the midst of a battle with terminal breast cancer, caring for a new baby, a 3-year-old and 7-year-old at home. However, she continued to work full-time with Pat until Pat left the school district (and I went with her to work at the National Center on Education and the Economy). Tanya then stayed on in the Saint Paul Public Schools for several months to ensure a smooth transition from Pat's administration.

Tanya and I often talked about whether or not she should continue working after she was diagnosed with stage 4 cancer. She chose to do so mostly because she believed so deeply in the work that Pat was leading. She also kept working because of the personal support she received from Pat, Rosie, and many others in the Saint Paul Public Schools.

Patricia Harvey was a unique mix of introvert and extrovert, humble and proud, casual and informal, intellectual and practical. When Pat arrived in Saint Paul after a career in the Chicago public schools driving a new Jaguar with vanity license plate (always PAH), many people both within and beyond the school district didn't quite know what to make of her.

Pat Harvey didn't fit the traditional Minnesota model of a school system leader. She seemed to some a bit distant and even imperial at times, but over the years they came to know her as a leader who was passionately committed to ensuring that all students received top quality instruction. The phrase "instructional leader" gets used a lot in education these days. Pat embodied that type of leadership better than anyone I have ever known.

The language Pat used as a leader in Saint Paul two decades ago would not sound rooted in "equity" to some today because she always avoided pitting parts of the district and the community against each other. She would often say to Tanya and me that while she understood the anger that people justifiably felt about injustices and inequities within the system, when families who have resources and options stop sending their children to an urban school district, you end up being Detroit or Chicago. I remember after one school board meeting at which some of the people who spoke at public comment seemed to be trying to educate Pat about the challenges of working in urban education, she said to Tanya and me, "The last school I was principal of in Chicago was 100% African-American and 98% of the kids qualified for free or reduced price lunch. When I say that we should set high academic expectations for all kids, I know that it can be done because I have done it."

Kent Pekel

45

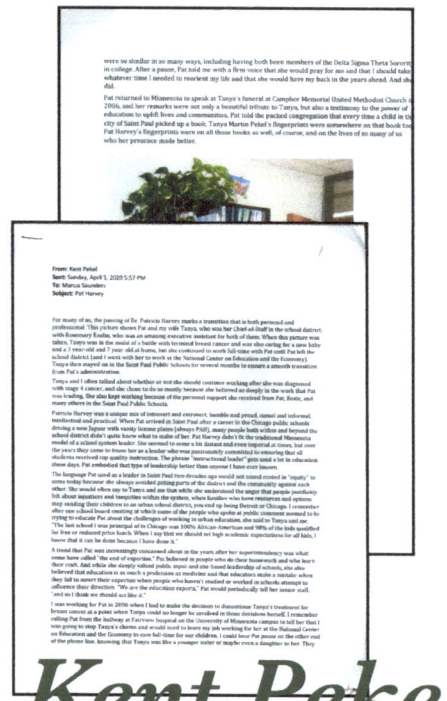

I was working for Pat in 2006 when l had to' make the decision to discontinue Tanya's treatment for breast cancer at a point when Tanya could no longer be involved in those decisions herself. I remember calling Pat from the hallway at Fairview hospital on the University of Minnesota campus to tell her that I was going to stop Tanya's chemo and would need to leave my job working for her at the National Center on Education and the Economy to care full-time for our children. I could hear Pat pause on the other end of the phone line, knowing that Tanya was like a younger sister or maybe even a daughter to her. They were so similar in so many ways, including having both been members of the Delta Sigma Theta Sorority in college. After a pause, Pat told me with a firm voice that she would pray for me and that I should take whatever time I needed to reorient my life and that she would have my back in the years ahead. And she did.

Pat returned to Minnesota to speak at Tanya's funeral at Camphor Memorial United Methodist Church in 2006, and her remarks were not only a beautiful tribute to Tanya, but also a testimony to the power of education to uplift lives and communities. Pat told the packed congregation that every time a child in the city of Saint Paul picked up a book, Tanya Martin Pekel's fingerprints were somewhere on that book too.

Pat Harvey's fingerprints were on all those books as well, of course, and on the lives of so many of us who her presence made better.

Remembering Tanya

"Remember me when I am gone away,
Gone far away into the silent land;
When you can no more hold me by the hand,
Nor I half turn to go, yet turning stay,
Remember me when no more, day by day."

-Christina Rosetti

For Tanya, it all began when she was a busy, talkative and energetic little girl around five or six years old, who just enjoyed coming to my home, along with her sister Terrie… just to READ my books. Of course, the books were arranged in specific categories on the bookshelf. And….knowing Tanya….she always managed to "find" the shelf with the "Children's books, as she selected not one… two… or three….but five books at a time to avoid going to the bookshelf for more. This was indeed a "Reading" moment for Tanya as she relaxed on the Red Rug with her little head propped upon a pillow and just enjoyed the magic moment of reading.

When asked what she had read, she immediately gave a step-by-step narrative in sequential order about the story. She was quite a mathematical whiz also, with high critical thinking skills. She was a gifted young child with a "thirst for learning. Based on those observations from one visit to another, I immediately surmised that Tanya was going to excel in everything she did and would become one of our community's most outstanding "treasures". And….that she was!

Maud P. Newbold

As time passed, Tanya was totally immersed in dance classes, music classes, honors and drama classes, and on her way to becoming one of Miami-Dade County's Merit Scholarship Winners.

However, during her high school years, she was masterful in scheduling time to volunteer her service to many "At-Risk-Children in the community. She was indeed a leader and scholar in her own right; but never failed to commit herself to others.

As a Congressional Page in High School, she got the "bug" for public service. Throughout her teenage years, she taught music, drama, dance and Sunday School to children as an Inner-City Ministry. In addition, she volunteered as a tutor and a mentor for "At-Risk-Youth". These activities were typical of Tanya, for she was indeed a "doer". She was devoted to family and led by quiet and dignified example. Our Tanya was an intelligent young woman of humble roots and great accomplishments. Her goal was to help "America" fulfill its great potential.

Yes…this was the little girl, who used to sit on the "red" carpet reading her books for hours and hours, who was selected as a White House Fellow by President Bill Clinton in 1995 with the assignment of Special Assistant to Secretary of Education Richard Riley.

Remembering Tanya

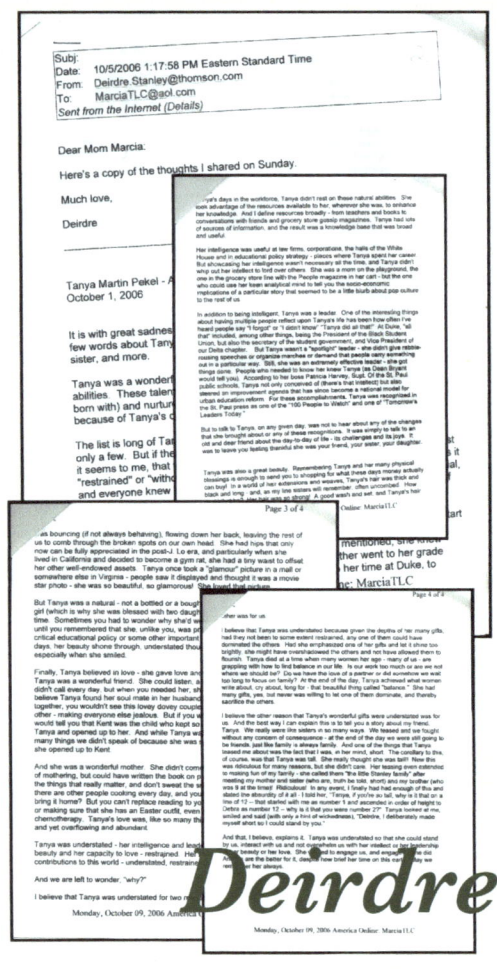

Deirdre Stanley

Deidre and Tanya were roommates at Duke and remained best friends. Both went to law school. Deidre is General Council at Estee Lauder

Dear Mom Marcia:
Here's a copy of the thoughts I shared on Sunday.

Much love,
Deirdre

Tanya Martin Pekel - An Understated, Excellent Life
October 1, 2006

It is with great sadness, but with a wonderful sense of privilege, that I will say a few words about Tanya Elayne Martin Pekel, my dear friend, my soror, my line sister, and more.

Tanya was a wonderful person. She was blessed with many talents and abilities. These talents and abilities were both a result of nature (some she was born with) and nurture (from her mother Marcia, her father Montez, and indeed because of Tanya's own desire to expand her mind and to grow).

The list is long of Tanya's many wonderful qualities, and I have time to mention only a few. But if there is one theme that seems to run throughout them, at least it seems to me, that theme would be "understated" - or as the dictionary defines it "restrained" or "without obvious emphasis or embellishment." Tanya was special and everyone knew it. And she didn't have to shout or draw attention to herself for that to be so.

Where to start when talking about Tanya? It's hard, but I think you'd have to start with her intelligence - Tanya was very, very smart. Naturally so. She could grasp things really quickly. Just about any subject you mentioned, she knew something about. But from the days when Tanya's mother went to her grade school to demand that she be put in the gifted class, to her time at Duke, to Tanya's days in the workforce, Tanya didn't rest on these natural abilities. She took advantage of the resources available to her, wherever she was, to enhance her knowledge. And I define resources broadly - from teachers and books to conversations with friends and grocery store gossip magazines. Tanya had lots of sources of information, and the result was a knowledge base that was broad and useful.

Her intelligence was useful at law firms, corporations, the halls of the White House and in educational policy strategy - places where Tanya spent her career. But showcasing her intelligence wasn't necessary all the time, and Tanya didn't whip out her intellect to lord over others. She was a mom on the playground, the one in the grocery store line with the People magazine in her cart - but the one who could use her keen analytical mind to tell you the socio-economic implications of a particular story that seemed to be a little blurb about pop culture to the rest of us.

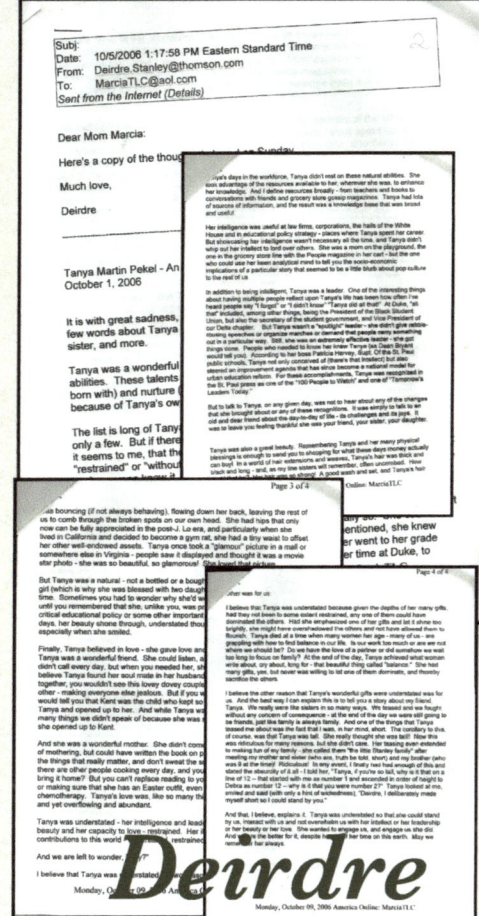

Deirdre Stanley

Deidre and Tanya were roommates at Duke and remained best friends. Both went to law school. Deidre is General Council at Estee Lauder

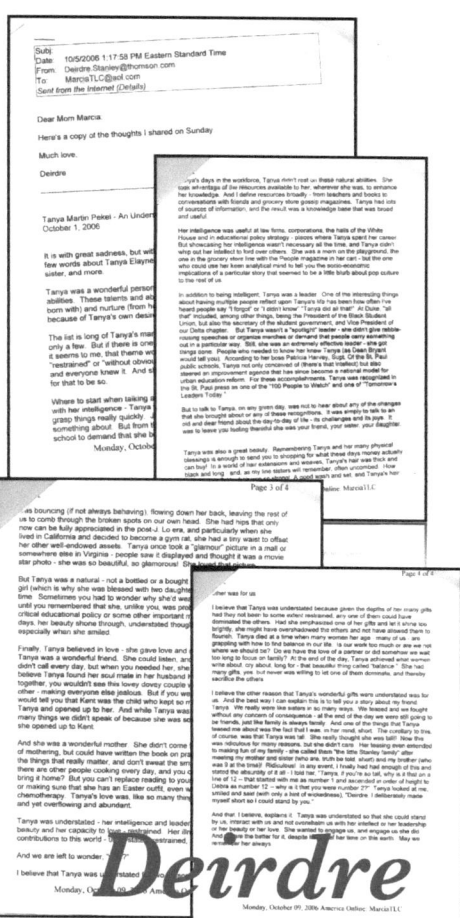

Deirdre Stanley

"feeling thankful she was your friend"

"she was a wonderful mother"

"Tanya was understated"

In addition to being intelligent, Tanya was a leader. One of the interesting things about having multiple people reflect upon Tanya's life has been how often I've heard people say, "I forgot" or "I didn't know" "Tanya did all that!"

At Duke, "all that" included, among other things, being the President of the Black Student Union, but also the secretary of the student government, and Vice President of our Delta chapter. But Tanya wasn't a "spotlight" leader. She didn't give rabble..rousing speeches or organize marches or demand that people carry something out in a particular way. Still, she was an extremely effective leader - she got things done. People who needed to know her knew. (as Dean Bryant would tell you). According to her boss Patricia Harvey, Supt. of the St. Paul public schools, Tanya not only conceived (there's that intellect) but also steered an improvement agenda that has since become a national model for urban education reform. For these accomplishments, Tanya was recognized in the St. Paul press as one of the "100 People to Watch" and one of "Tomorrow's Leaders Today."

To talk to Tanya on any given day, was not to hear about any of the changes that she brought about or any of these recognitions. It was simply to talk to an old and dear friend about the day-to-day of life - its challenges and its joys. It was to leave you feeling thankful she was your friend, your sister, your daughter.

Tanya was also a great beauty. Remembering Tanya and her many physical blessings is enough to send you to shopping for what these days money actually can buy! In a world of hair extensions and weaves, Tanya's hair was thick, black and long - and, as my line sisters will remember, often uncombed. How could that be? Her hair was so strong! A good wash and set, and Tanya's hair was bouncing (if not always behaving), flowing down her back, leaving the rest of us to comb through the broken spots on our own head. She had hips that only now can be fully appreciated in the post J-Lo era, and particularly when she lived in California and decided to become a gym rat, she had a tiny waist to offset her other well-endowed assets. Tanya once took a "glamour" picture in a mall or somewhere else in Virginia - people saw it displayed and thought it was a movie star photo - she was so beautiful, so glamorous! She loved that picture.

But Tanya was a natural - not a bottled or a bought -- beauty. She wasn't a girlie girl (which is why she was blessed with two daughters who are). She didn't have time. Sometimes you had to wonder why she'd wear those socks with that outfit - until you remembered that she, unlike you, was probably contemplating some critical educational policy or some other important matter. But even on those days, her beauty shone through, understated though it might have been, especially when she smiled.

Finally, Tanya believed in love - she gave love and she was loved in return. Tanya was a wonderful friend. She could listen, and she could empathize. She didn't call every day, but when you needed her, she was wholly there. I really believe Tanya found her soulmate in her husband Kent. If you saw them together, you wouldn't see this lovey-dovey couple with their hands all over each other - making everyone else jealous. But if you were to ask Kent's mother, she would tell you that Kent was the child who kept so much inside, until he met Tanya and opened up to her. And while Tanya was my best friend, there are so many things we didn't speak of because she was so often so insular -- and yet she opened up to Kent.

And she was a wonderful mother. She didn't come from the Donna Reed school of mothering, but could have written the book on practical parenting - focus on the things that really matter, and don't sweat the small stuff. Why cook when there are other people cooking every day, and you can buy their good food and bring it home? But you can't replace reading to your child, or rubbing her back, or making sure that she has an Easter outfit, even when you are on chemotherapy. Tanya's love was, like so many things about Tanya, understated, yet overflowing and abundant.

Tanya was understated - her intelligence and leadership - understated. Her beauty and her capacity to love - understated. Her illness - understated. Her contributions to this world .. understated, restrained, sometimes not obvious.

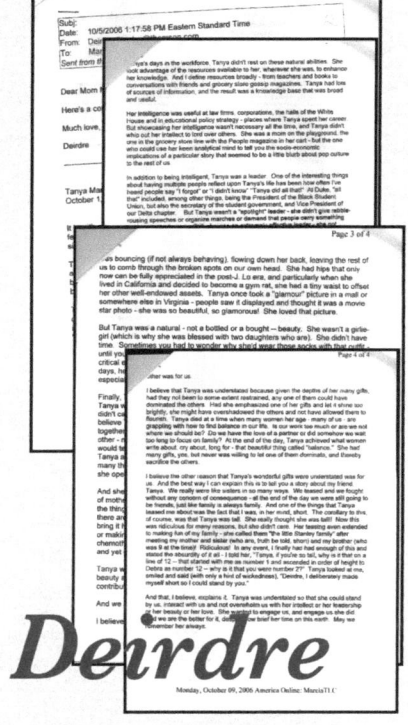

Deirdre Stanley

"feeling thankful she was your friend"

"she was a wonderful mother"

"Tanya was understated"

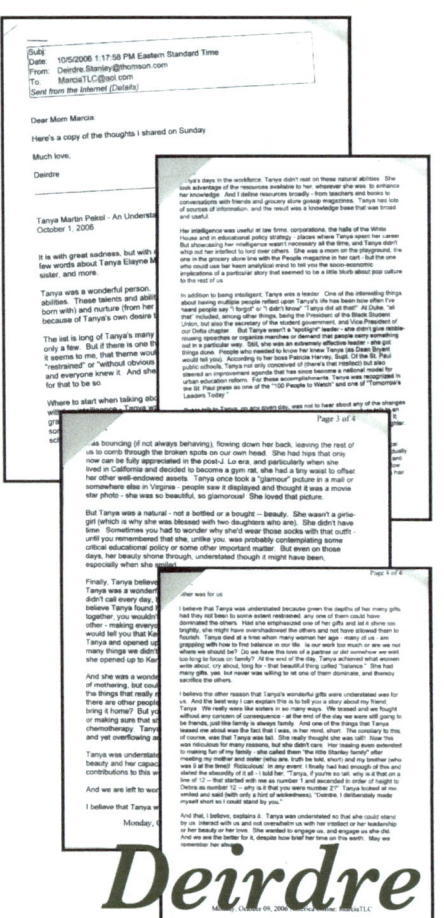

Deirdre Stanley

And we are left to wonder, "why?"

I believe that Tanya was understated for two reasons - one was for her, and the other was for us.

I Believe that Tanya was understated because given the depths of her many gifts, had they not been to some extent restrained, any one of them could have dominated the others. Had she emphasized one of her gifts and let it shine too brightly, she might have overshadowed the others and not have allowed them to flourish.

Tanya died at a time when many women her age - many of us - are grappling with how to find balance in our life. Is our work too much or are we not where we should be? Do we have the love of a partner or did somehow we wait too long to focus on family? At the end of the day, Tanya achieved what women write about, cry about, long for - that beautiful thing called "balance."

She had many gifts, yes, but never was willing to let one of them dominate, and thereby sacrifice the others.

I believe the other reason that Tanya's wonderful gifts were understated was for us. And the best way I can explain this is to tell you a story about my friend, Tanya. We really were like sisters in so many ways. We teased and we fought without any concern of consequence - at the end of the day we were still going to be friends, just like family is always family. And one of the things that Tanya teased me about was the fact that I was, in her mind, short. The corollary to this, of course, was that Tanya was tall. She really thought she was tall!! Now this was ridiculous for many reasons, but she didn't care. Her teasing even extended to making fun of my family - she called them "the little Stanley family" after meeting my mother and sister (who are, truth be told, short) and my brother (who was nine at the time)! Ridiculous! In any event, I finally had had enough of this and stated the absurdity of it all - I told her, "Tanya, if you're so tall, why is it that on a line of 12 -- that started with me as number 1 and ascended in order of height to Debra as number 12 -- why is it that you were number 2?" Tanya looked at me, smiled and said (with only a hint of wickedness), "Deirdre, I deliberately made myself short so I could stand by you.

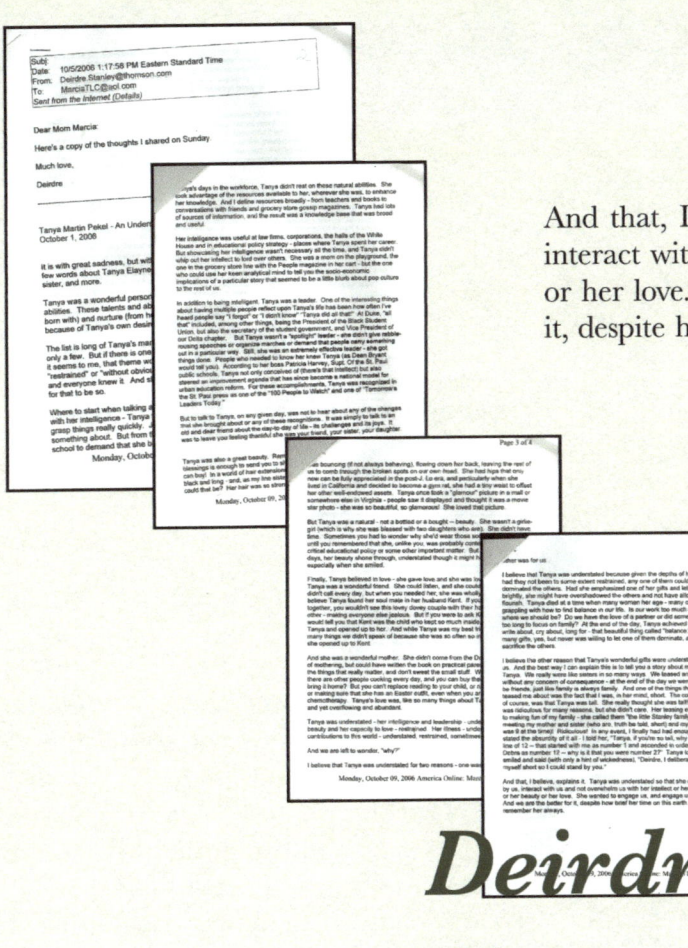

And that, I believe, explains it. Tanya was understated so that she could stand by us, interact with us and not overwhelm us with her intellect or her leadership or her beauty or her love. She wanted to engage us, and engage us she did. And we are the better for it, despite how brief her time on this earth. May we remember her always.

Deirdre Stanley

Remembering Tanya

Introduction to Memorial Service For Tanya Martin Pekel
Jerri Dunston   October 1, 2006,
Mary Lou Cultural Center, Duke University

Jerri Dunston

We are here today to celebrate the memory of Tanya Martin Pekel. As many of you are aware, Tanya passed away in May of this year after a valiant battle with breast cancer. Many of us didn't get an opportunity to go to her funeral in Minneapolis and it was important for us to take some time today to remember Tanya and the wonderful contributions she made to our lives and to the Duke Community.

Tanya was a Renaissance woman. While she was here at Duke, she truly availed herself of everything that Duke has to offer. She loved the arts. She performed with Dance Black (and there will be a tribute to her today from the group). She sang with the group formerly known as the Modern Black Mass Choir (and the successor, United in Praise, will perform here today as well). Tanya loved poetry, especially Maya Angelou, and she wrote poems for Prometheus Black (a journal formerly published by black students at Duke).

Tanya participated in Greek life. We pledged Delta Sigma Theta in the Spring of 1984. And Lambda Omega took pride then (and takes pride now) in serving the Durham community.

Most of all, Tanya was a leader. She served as the President of the Black Student Alliance from 1986-1986 and also served on the President's Honor Council.

After she graduated in 1986, Tanya went on to attend law school here at Duke. She became a lawyer and later applied to become a White House Fellow. I don't know how many of you know about the Fellowship program. The program is designed to identify and foster the development of future leaders in public service. Fellows are assigned to work day-to-day with high-level officials in the executive branch for a year. After the fellowship, they are expected to go back to their communities and implement the policies and programs they have learned about or developed.

Hundreds and hundreds of people apply to the program every year from all over the country, and the White House only chooses about 20 or fewer of the applicants to participate in the program. Tanya applied, and in 1995 was accepted and worked with the Secretary of Education. She also met Kent, her future husband, who also was serving as a Fellow.

After marrying Kent, Tanya moved to Minneapolis and worked on fulfilling the promise of her Fellowship by serving as the Chief of Staff to the Superintendent of Schools in St. Paul. Tanya believed that where there was a will within our community to have our children educated, there had to be a way to accomplish that goal. And she turned her considerable talents toward achieving educational equality, opportunities, and achievement in St. Paul. She and Kent had three beautiful children.

Tanya wasn't just a Renaissance woman, or a lawyer, or an educator, or a wife, or a mother, or a daughter or a sister. Tanya was one of the smartest people I have ever known. She knew a whole lot about a lot of stuff! And she could be so funny and so silly. And most of all, she was incredibly pragmatic. Tanya wouldn't accept a whole lot of foolishness. She would cut to the heart of the matter while others around her were twirling around in circles. If you didn't know Tanya, though, you'd probably think she was ditzy. You'd be over here in the moment, but Tanya's mind truly would be working somewhere on a level that you couldn't go or hadn't achieved yet.

I remember Tanya at sorority meetings. We would be arguing and fussing over something that was completely foolish. Sometimes we were angry at each other and ready to throw down. Tanya would put her head down on the table and put her arm over her head. You wouldn't know whether she was paying attention or asleep. Finally, she would have had enough! She'd put her arm down, raise her head up and say something that would stop the silliness in its tracks. You couldn't predict what would come out of her mouth!

Sometimes it would be something light and silly to cut the tension. Sometimes it would be something so profound that it might take you a week or two to really get it. You just never knew in advance which one it would be.

I'm going to share one last story that epitomizes Tanya and her indomitable spirit. Tanya and Deirdre visited Washington, D.C. in February of this year. Deirdre was there on business and Tanya and Kent came for a reunion of White House Fellows. Tanya and Deirdre stayed an extra night, and a small group of sorors went over to Georgetown to hang out on Saturday afternoon. We were walking down Wisconsin Avenue toward M Street at around 1 or 2 in the afternoon. Those of you who are familiar with Georgetown know that the intersection of Wisconsin and M Street is one of the busiest intersections in the city in terms of pedestrian and vehicular traffic. On weekends, the traffic is particularly bad.

Well, apparently Nicole Kidman was shooting some kind of movie in Georgetown that day. As we walked toward M Street, we walked into a crowd of about 20 or 30 people. A production assistant from the movie (a young girl in her early twenties with a wireless headphone on her head) had stopped the crowd from walking down the sidewalk. She had her hand out and was saying, "I'm sorry, but you can't go over there."

We stood in the crowd for several minutes, getting information about the filming of the movie. Then, of course, we all began to debate whether the movie company had the right to come to Georgetown on the busiest shopping day of the week at the busiest hour of the day and try to keep people from walking down a public sidewalk and keep cars from driving along a public street. Some people (apparently from the neighborhood) had the nerve to say that it was a good thing that the company was filming in the neighborhood because it would bring business and money. I was incredulous and just had to note that, of all the neighborhoods in D.C., Georgetown was the one that least needed that kind of money or attention. Something made us look up from the debate and all of a sudden, we saw Tanya marching her way past that girl wearing the wireless headphones. There was nothing that girl could do to stop her! When the rest of us (sorors) realized that Tanya was marching past the

Jerri Dunston

assistant, we marched right behind her. And when the rest of the crowd saw us marching past the assistant, they did the same. Soon we were all marching down the sidewalk and going on about our business!

After we caught up to Tanya, we asked her why she had gone past the assistant. Tanya said, "Who is she to tell me where I can and can't go? She works for a living every day just like me!"

So, I ask all of you today to pledge that you won't let someone put up a hand and try to stop your progress! I ask each of you to remember that no one can tell you that you can't go where you want or achieve what you most desire. I also challenge the students at Duke today to make the most out of all that the school has to offer. If we can remember and do these things, that would be the greatest tribute we can pay to Tanya.

Jerri Dunston

Remembering Tanya

KNOWING TANYA ELAYNE MARTIN PEKEL

~My Personal Memoir~

As I was working on these remarks yesterday morning, I heard John Hope Franklin discuss his recently published autobiography. During his comments he differentiated between an autobiography and a memoir. An autobiography is a thoroughly researched, substantive account of one's life while a memoir is a collection of remembrances. My comments today will reveal for you my thoughts and remembrances of Tanya.

She: My parents went to Hampton Institute. - Really, I did too. What were their names?
She: (Proudly and distinctly) Marcia Johnson and Montez Martin. That night I called my Hampton friends to tell them about Tanya, Marcia and Montez's daughter.

The next installment focuses on Tanya's coming to Duke. Once I learned Duke had been successful in recruiting her, I made it my business to watch her and try to shepherd her. It was not long before I realized that Tanya was her own person in her own right and she was very able to navigate Duke. She was always direct, forthright, and without any show of pomposity. There was a wide horizon before her-both at Duke and beyond Duke-and she was going to travel towards it. Whenever she talked, it was always about the next steps and making progress. Throughout, she was mature, sensible, and totally delightful.

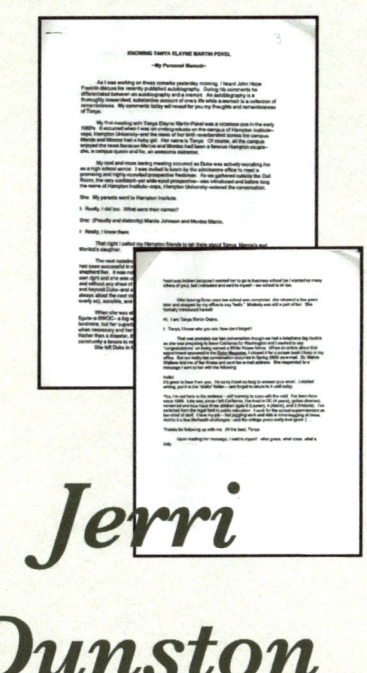

Jerri Dunston

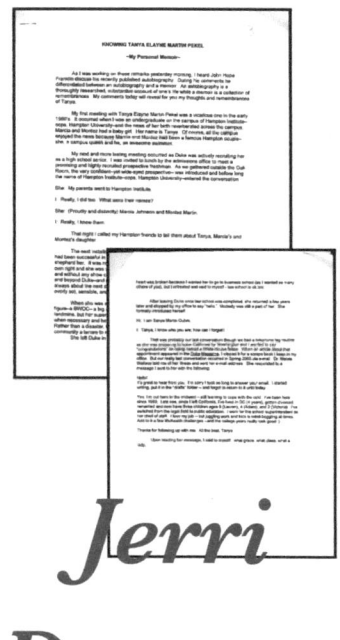

Jerri Dunston

When she was elected, BSA president, I was able to witness Tanya as a public figure-a BWOC- a big woman on campus. The BSA presidency could easily be a land mine, but her superb mind allowed for clear thinking and her ability to assimilate when necessary and her warm and respected manner led to no disasters or criticism. Rather than a disaster, the presidency furthered her development and gave the Duke community a tenure to remember.

She left Duke in May 1986 only to return in August 1986 for law school. My heart was broken because I wanted her to go to business school (as I wanted so many others of you), but I retreated and said to myself - law school is OK too.

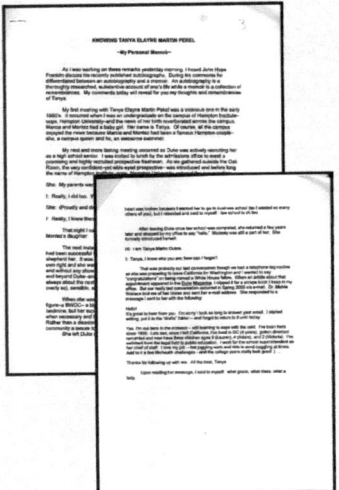

After leaving Duke once law school was completed, she returned a few years later and stopped by my office to say "hello." Modesty was still a part of her. She formally introduced herself:

Tanya: Hi, I am Tanya Martin Oubre.

I: Tanya, I know who you are; how can I forget!!

That was probably our last conversation though we had a telephone tag routine as she was preparing to leave California for Washington and I wanted to say "congratulations" on being named a White House Fellow. When an article about that appointment appeared in the <u>Duke Magazine</u>, I clipped it for a scrapbook I keep in my office. But our really last conversation occurred in Spring 2005 via e-mail. Dr. Melvia Wallace told me of her illness and sent her e-mail address. She responded to a message I sent to her with the following:

Hello!
It's great to hear from you. I'm sorry I took so long to answer your email. I started writing, put it in the "drafts" folder - and forgot to return to it until today.

Yes, I'm out here in the midwest- still learning to cope with the cold. I've been here since 1999. Let's see, since I left California, I've lived in DC (4 years), gotten divorced, remarried and now have three children ages 9 (Lauren), 4 (Adam), and 2 (Victoria). I've switched from the legal field to public education. I work for the school superintendent as her chief of staff. I love my job -- but juggling work and kids is mind-boggling at times. Add to it a few life/health challenges --and the college years really look good :) ...

Thanks for following up with me.
All the best, Tanya

Honoring Tanya

Rick Scott Approves Legislators' Road and Bridge Dedications

By
JIM TURNER
April 7, 2012 - 6:00pm

Tanya Martin Oubre Pekel Street. Oubre Pekel was a Miami native who served as an associate director of Education and Policy Planning in the Clinton White House. She passed away on May 22, 2006. State Road 932/N.E. 103rd Street 169 between N.W. 3rd Avenue and N.E. 6th Avenue in Miami-Dade County.

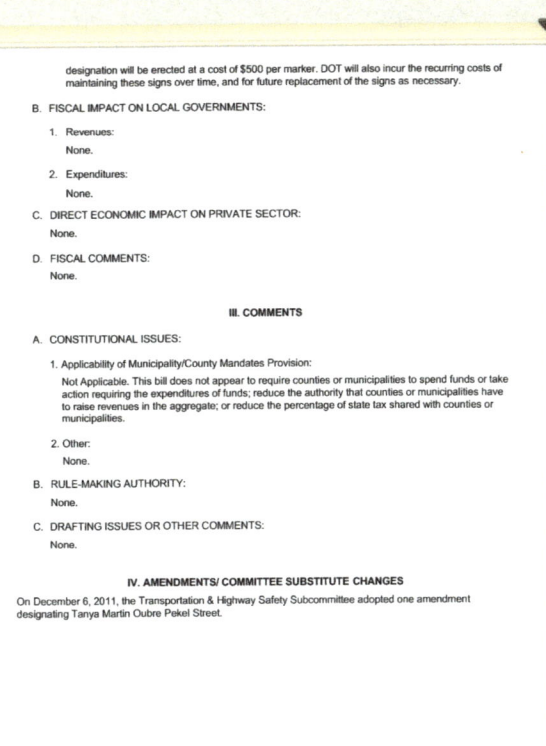

Unimagined Impact

Hon. Kendrick B. Meek

KENDRICK B. MEEK
FLORIDA

HOUSE OF REPRESENTATIVES
WASHINGTON, D. C. 20515

Congressional Record

PROCEEDINGS AND DEBATES OF THE 110th CONGRESS, FIRST SESSION

House of Representatives

HON. KENDRICK B. MEEK
OF FLORIDA
IN THE HOUSE OF REPRESENTATIVES

Mr. MEEK of Florida. Madame Speaker: Today I rise to pay tribute to the life and legacy of the late Tanya Martin Oubre Pekel of Miami, Florida.

On Monday, May, 22, 2006, this great pioneering young woman succumbed to a nearly three-year battle with breast cancer at the age of 41. Her untimely passing will truly leave a deep void in our midst.

A native of Miami, Mrs. Martin Pekel was born on October 3, 1964. She graduated with honors from North Miami Senior High School. During that time she served as a page for U.S. Representative William Lehman and worked as a clerk for attorney H.T. Smith. Later, she earned a bachelor's degree from Duke University, and in 1989 she received her juris doctorate from Duke's School of Law.

Mrs. Martin Pekel continued on to work as a corporate attorney before being appointed a White House Fellow by President Clinton in 1995. Under this appointment, she became an Associate Director of Education and Policy Planning in the White House. In 1999, she accepted the position of Chief of Staff to Superintendent Patricia Harvey of Saint Paul Public Schools in St. Paul, Minnesota and served in the position for six years. In 2003, she was named one of that city's up and coming leaders.

Her commitment to public service and her community was evident from a young age. Throughout her life, she taught music, drama, dance, and Sunday school to children in an inner-city ministry. In addition, she volunteered as a tutor and mentor for at-risk youth.

Tanya Martin Oubre Pekel's life was a triumph. She was blessed with a loving family who took pleasure in every aspect of her life and her interests. Though she was taken from them far too early in her life, memories of her will live on in the heart of her family forever.

I pay tribute to Mrs. Martin Pekel, and I mourn her loss. She will be missed by all who knew her. I offer my heartfelt condolences to her family—her mother, Marcia Saunders; father, Montez Martin Jr.; husband, Kent; daughters, Lauren and Victoria; son, Adam; sisters, Terrie Rayburn and Emily Martin; brother, Montez C. Martin III; and grandmother, Elise Martin.

Street Dedication

Street Co-Designation Ceremony
in honor of
Tanya Martin Pekel, Esq.

Friday, March 1, 2013
10 a.m.
Miami Shores Elementary School
10351 N.E. 5th Avenue, Miami Shores, Florida 33138

Mistress of Ceremonies	Ms. Stephanie Bromfield
Pledge of Allegiance	
Solo - "America The Beautiful"	Mrs. Euphemia Ferguson
Invocation	The Reverend Cannon J. Kenneth Major Rector Emeritas The Episcopal Church of the Incarnation
Welcome	Ms. Tricia Fernandez, Principal Miami Shores Elementary School
	Dr. Dorothy Bendross-Mindingall School Board Member, District 2 Miami-Dade County Public Schools,
Purpose	Mrs. Daphne D. Campbell State Representative, District 108 Florida House of Representatives

Reflections and Remarks

Ms. Joyce Postell	District Director for U.S. Congresswoman Frederica Wilson 24th District of Florida
Dr. Anna Price	Executive Minister, Universal Truth Center Former University of Miami Administrator
Ms. Maud Newbold	Godmother Charter Member, Delta Sigma Theta Sorority, Inc. Dade County Alumnae Chapter
Response	Ms. Marcia Saunders and Montez Martin, Jr.

Video Presentation

Unveiling of the Street Sign

Closing Remarks	State Representative Daphne D. Campbell

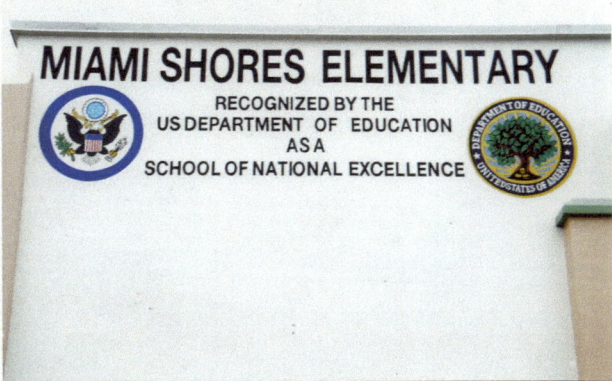

A Street Named In Her Honor

Tanya

"On Friday, March 1 at Miami Shores Elementary School, 103 Street and N.E. Sixth Avenue in Miami Shore, family members, friends and others gathered for the street renaming in honor of Tanya Martin Pekel (Oct. 3, 1964 - May 22, 2006), who died following a 2 1/2 year battle with breast cancer. The daughter of Marcia Saunders and a loving mother of three, she was a former White House fellow, corporate attorney, domestic policy expert and urban-school innovator." South Florida Times

A Street Named In Her Honor

Tanya Martin Pekel Timeline

1964 - October 3 Tanya Martin was born to Montez and Marcia Martin

1970 - Mother relocated family to Miami

1982 - Tanya graduated with honors

1982 -1986 Attended Duke University - AB Economics

1986 - Duke Class representative

1986 - University of Miami's Upward Bound teacher

1986 - 1989 Duke University School of Law

1989 - Corporate attorney at Simpson, Thatcher & Bartlett on Wall Street

1990 - Moved to Los Angelos, CA and worked as an attorney

1990 - Married Derek Oubre - One daughter - Lauren

1995 -1996 White House Fellow - President Bill Clinton

1999 - Married Kent Pekel - son, Adam and daughter, Victoria

2006 - May 22 Tanya passed away at age 41

Her Legacy Continues

Kent, Victoria, Lauren, Adam

Adam, Lauren, Victoria, Marcia

Wendell & Terrie,
Taylor, Sydney, and Carter Rayburn

Tanya Highlights

* Served as a Florida Page in Tallahassee

* Served as congressional page for Hon. William Lehman in Washington, DC

* Appointed by President William Jefferson Clinton as a 1995-1996 White House Fellow. A highly competitive and prestigious award. Former awardees include former HUD Secretary Henry Cisneros, historian Doris Kearns Goodwin, and former Joint Chiefs of Staff Chairman Colin Powell. The award is based on academic, professional and civic achievement.

The program's purpose is to identify and foster the development of future leaders in public service who will take the lessons of federal service back to their communities and make a difference in their communities. Fellows are assigned to work day to day with high level officials in the executive branch for a year. Following the fellowship they are expected to return to their communities and implement the policies and programs they have learned about or developed.

Tanya was given the assignment of special assistant to Secretary of Education Richard Riley. When the fellowship ended, the head of Clinton's Domestic Policy Council asked Tanya to serve as the President's Associate Director for Education Policy and Planning. "In the role she helped shape the key education initiatives of the turn of the century—class size reduction, volunteer service, school construction, bilingual education, and charter school development." Her fondest memory of working at the White House: she got a chance to ride on Air Force One.

* For her work with School Supt. Harvey and her model for urban education reform, the St. Paul Press recognized her as one of "100 People to Watch" and one of "Tomorrow's Leaders Today."

* Sponsored by State Representative Daphne Campbell, a street at 1 Miami Shores Elementary School, 103 Street & NE Sixth Avenue in Miami Shores was renamed in Tanya's honor. It was renamed Tanya Martin Oubre Pekel Rd. The street designation ceremony was held on March 1, 2013. To commemorate her legacy of reading, a book giveaway and tutoring initiative for underserved communities was also launched.

Resources To Explore

WEBSITES:

Florida Encyclopedia of Law:
https://florida.lawi.us/tanya-martin-oubre-pekel-street/
http://laws.flrules.org/2012/228
https://legiscan.com/FL/bill/H0533/2012

Glimpses of Tanya Martin Pekel
https://www.youtube.com/watch?v=kSDBOWeVhJc

House of Representatives Staff Analysis
https://www.flsenate.gov/Session/Bill/2012/533/Analyses/h0533a.THSS.PDF - Summary
https://www.flsenate.gov/Session/Bill/2012/0533/BillText/c1/PDF
https://www.flsenate.gov/Session/Bill/2012/0533/BillText/Filed/HTML - Text

South Florida Times
http://www.sfltimes.com/uncategorized/road-is-named-for-pekel-2
http://www.sfltimes.com/uncategorized/new-briefs

Saint Paul Issues Forum
http://forums.e-democracy.org/groups/stpaul-issues/messages/topic/1aYIaScX3fL8qc7kTAZck1

Saint Paul Public Schools
https://www.dol.gov/sites/dolgov/files/olms/regs/compliance/cba/pdf/cbrp1933.pdf
https://www.dol.gov/sites/dolgov/files/olms/regs/compliance/cba/pdf/cbrp1934.pdf

Berkley
https://irle.berkeley.edu/digital-collection/bargaining/pdf/0190.pdf

White House Fellows Projects 1995/1996:

http://www.whitehousefellowsproject.org/
whitehousefellowsproject.rice.edu/Default2568.html?id=49

Of Arms & the Law
https://armsandthelaw.com/archives/2015/09/clinton_archive.php#comment-55374

Delta Sigma Theta
https://issuu.com/progressivegreek/docs/dst_spring_2009/77

Search Institute
https://www.search-institute.org/about-us/staff/kent-pekel/
https://blog.search-institute.org/expectations-assumptions-white-mans-experience-racial-profiling

Thank You
For Preserving Her Story

Deirdre Stanley
Dorothy Fields
Jerri Dunston
Duke University
Hon. Kendrick Meeks
Kent Pekel
Marcia M. Saunders
Miami Shores Elementary
Maud Newbold
US President Clinton
Clinton White House Fellows

Compiled by
Ersula K Odom

As CEO of Sula Too LLC, Ersula K. Odom is on a mission to preserve cultural history in any form possible. As such she is a publisher, legacy wall designer, legacy writer, and living history performer. She is also founder of Ersula's History Shop and the non-profit company Rescuing History, Inc. Collectively, all of her skills lead to preparing your story, rather average and ordinary or extraordinary, to take its rightful place in our history.

Ersula combines research, life and professional experiences of rural living, college life, fortune 500 corporate management, spirituality, family, entrepreneurship, sales, genealogy, and publishing, to deliver relative multi-generational and multi-cultural products and services.

www.sulatoo.com/publishing

Other books by Ersula K Odom:
At Sula's Feet
The Doris Ross Reddick Story
Miss Lizzy's Story
African Americans of Tampa
Pamala McCoy-A Shero's Story
Create Your Signature Book In A Weekend
Rogers Park Golf Course
Rolanda McDuffie On Living Life As Intended

www.ingramcontent.com/pod-product-compliance
Lightning Source LLC
Chambersburg PA
CBHW041647160426
43209CB00019B/1849